LET'S CELEBRATE

Christopher Columbus

and His Voyage to the New World

by Robert Young
pictures by Arvis Stewart

Silver Press

Produced by Kirchoff/Wohlberg, Inc.
Text copyright © 1990 Kirchoff/Wohlberg, Inc.
Illustrations copyright © 1990 Arvis Stewart and
Kirchoff/Wohlberg, Inc.

Published by Silver Press, a division of Silver Burdett Press, Inc.
Simon & Schuster, Inc., Prentice Hall Bldg., Englewood Cliffs, NJ 07632

Printed in the United States of America

10 9 8 7 6   0671691040
10 9 8 7 6 5   0382394755

Library of Congress Cataloging-in-Publication Data
Young Robert, 1951–
Christopher Columbus and the discovery of America / by Robert
Young: pictures by Arvis Stewart.
p. cm.—(Let's celebrate)
Summary: Describes the life of Christopher Columbus and how he
came to discover the New World.
1. Columbus, Christopher—Juvenile literature. 2. Explorers—
America—Biography—Juvenile literature. 3. Explorers—Spain—
Biography—Juvenile literature. 4. America—Discovery and
exploration—Spanish—Juvenile literature. [1. Columbus,
Christopher. 2. Explorers. 3. America—Discovery and exploration.]
I. Stewart, Arvis L., ill. II. Title. III. Series.
E111.Y74 1990
970.01′5′092—dc20   89-70317
[B]   CIP
[92]   AC

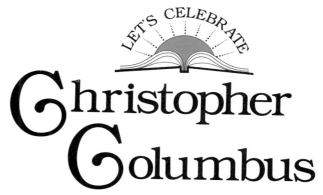

Let's Celebrate
Christopher Columbus

and His Voyage to the New World

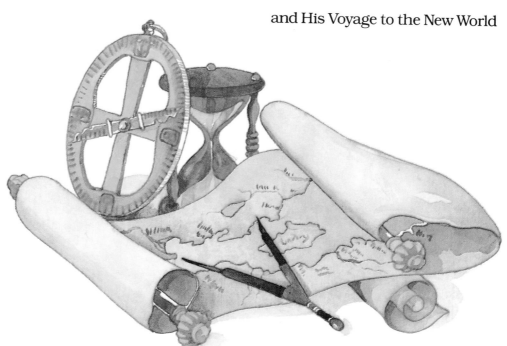

Young Christopher

Christopher Columbus looked out at the busy port of Genoa, Italy. Tall-masted sailing ships filled the harbor. Christopher loved to look at the ships. And he never grew tired of watching the busy sailors who worked on them.

"Christopher!" his father said sharply. "Come away from the window. You'll never learn to be a weaver if you don't pay attention."

"I'm sorry," said Christopher as he turned away from the window. He stood by his father and watched him work the loom that made wool into cloth.

"I don't want to be a weaver," Christopher thought. "I'm not interested in making cloth. And I hate working in this small, dark weaving room."

Soon Christopher was gazing out the window again. A ship with wind-filled sails glided out to sea. "I'd love to work on a ship like that," he said to himself. "I'd love to be a sailor and travel to faraway lands."

6

Learning to Sail

A few years passed. Christopher was still working in his father's weaving shop. But he still dreamed of the time he could go to sea.

One day as Christopher and his father walked past a large ship in the harbor, his father said, "I love to weave, just as my father did. But I can see that weaving is not for you. Why don't you learn to be a sailor? Then you can sail on the ships that take my cloth to market. You will still be helping me."

Christopher was delighted. "I'll be the best sailor you've ever seen!" he promised.

Christopher couldn't wait to get out to sea. He wanted to watch the wind fill the sails. He wanted to feel the salt air on his face. And he wanted to learn all he could about ships and sailing.

Several years later, Christopher was talking to his brother Bartholomew. "I've learned all I can teach myself about sailing," Christopher said. "I need to work with sailors who can teach me more."

So he started working on large trading ships. He learned a lot from the older sailors. They taught him how to sail in storms. They showed him how to use a compass and to study the stars to find his way.

12

One day, the trading ship on which Christopher was sailing was attacked by a French warship. The warship's cannons roared. Cannonballs ripped into the trading ship's side. A great fire broke out. It spread throughout the ship. The ship began to sink. To save his life, Columbus jumped over the side and into the water. Although he was hurt and bleeding, he began to swim toward shore. When an oar floated by, Christopher grabbed hold of it. Sometimes swimming and sometimes resting on the oar, he finally reached the sandy shore of Portugal.

Christopher's brother Bartholomew was now living in Portugal. He was working as a mapmaker. As soon as Christopher felt well enough, he went to look for him.

Christopher told Bartholomew how his ship sank and how he swam to safety.

"I'm glad you are alive," Bartholomew said. "And now you are with me in Portugal. The best sailors in the world live here. You can learn a lot from them. And you can work with me. I will teach you to make maps."

Bartholomew showed Christopher a map of the world. Christopher's eyes grew wide. "Look at all the places to go," he said.

Bartholomew put his finger on the map. "This is a place you should go. You can find riches and spices and perfume here. It is called the Indies," he said.

Christopher smiled. "The Indies," he said. "Someday I will sail there."

The Great Plan

Christopher stayed in Portugal. He worked with Bartholomew in his mapmaking shop. During this time he learned how to read. He also studied geography, mathematics, and astronomy.

After a time he married a woman named Doña Felipa. They had a son and called him Diego.

One day Christopher told his wife about his plan to sail to the Indies. "The Indies are far to the east," he explained. "But, since I believe the world is round, I am sure if I sail west I will get there."

"That will bring you great honor. No one has ever sailed west to get to the Far East," said Doña Felipa.

"Yes, I will be the first," Christopher answered. "I have a new map that shows it is possible."

"But you have no ships," his wife said.

"Not yet," replied Christopher. "I have to find someone who will pay for my ships and crew. Perhaps the king of Portugal will help me."

Christopher went to the king of Portugal. He told him of his plan to sail west to reach the Indies. Then he asked for the money he needed to make the trip. The king thought about Columbus's plan. Finally, he said, "Your plan will never work. The journey is too long."

But Columbus didn't give up. He went to Spain to ask for money for his trip.

In Spain, Columbus met with the king and queen. "I believe I can reach the Indies by sailing west. Will you give me the ships and crew I need to prove I'm right?" he asked. "If you do, I will bring back riches for Spain."

The king and queen were interested in Columbus's plan. But they told him he would have to wait. "We want to ask our advisers what they think."

"He's crazy!" the advisers told the king and queen. "His plan will never work. The Indies are too far away. He will be lost at sea."

Columbus waited a long time. It was four years before the king and queen finally gave him their answer. "We will not give you ships and a crew. No one believes you can reach the Indies, and make it back again."

Some time later Columbus stood before the king and queen of Spain for a second time. Once more he asked for the ships and crew to sail to the Indies.

"What reward do you expect?" asked the king.

"I want to be called an admiral," said Christopher. "I want to be in charge of all the lands I find. And I want a share of the riches I bring back."

"You ask for too much," the king replied. "Our answer is no!"

Columbus was angry. He was sure that his plan would work. "I will try to get help from the king of France," he decided. He packed his saddle bags and started on his way.

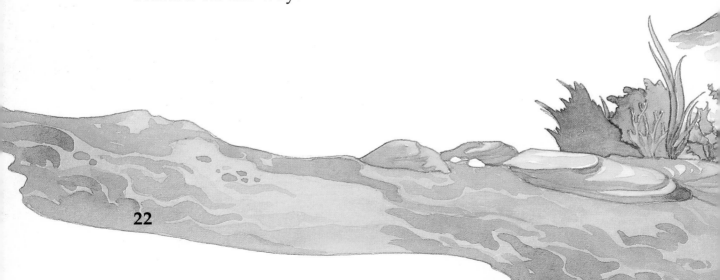

Then the queen's adviser told her that she and the king had made a mistake. He said they should give Columbus what he wanted. So the king and queen changed their minds and sent a messenger to find Columbus.

When the messenger caught up with Columbus he shouted, "The king and queen want you to come back. They've agreed to give you everything you want!"

"At last!" said Columbus. "I am going to sail west to reach the Indies."

The Voyage

It was early on a hot August morning in 1492. Columbus stood on the deck of the *Santa María*. His three ships were loaded and ready. His crew of ninety men was ready. And Columbus was ready, too. He was ready to use all his sailing skills. He was ready to sail where no one else had. ''Lift anchors!'' Columbus called. The *Niña*, the *Pinta*, and the *Santa María* set sail. They were on their way to the Indies.

Columbus leaned over the rail. He watched the bubbles the ship made in the water. They were floating by fast. Columbus smiled. He knew they would sail many miles that day.

Next he looked at his compass. He wanted to be sure the ships were sailing west. "Keep west!" he shouted. "Nothing but west."

The three ships kept sailing west. One morning, Columbus was working in his cabin. He was writing in his log. Each day, Columbus wrote about things he saw and the distance the ships traveled. He also kept a record of the winds and the currents.

Juan, the ship's master, came to the door. "There's trouble with the crew," Juan said.

Columbus looked up from his log. "What kind of trouble?" he asked.

"We have not seen land for three weeks," Juan told him. "Some men think they will never see land again. I am afraid for you, sir. The men are very angry. They want to throw you over the side."

"I will talk to them," said Columbus.

Columbus met with the crew. "Where are the Indies?" the men shouted. "When will we get there?"

"We've seen small birds. They are a sign that land is near. We'll sight land soon," Columbus promised.

They sailed for two more weeks. Still they did not
see land. One night as Columbus was walking on deck, he
saw a light to the west. It looked like a wax candle
bobbing up and down. He called for Pedro, one of the
king's men. Yes, Pedro saw the light, too. But by the time
other sailors looked, the light was gone.

Four hours later the men on the *Pinta* fired their
cannon. "That's it!" cried Columbus. "That's the signal. A
sailor on the *Pinta* has sighted land!"

The next morning, October 12, 1492, the sailors saw an island. It was big, with many trees and fruit. Some sailors rowed Columbus to shore in a small boat. He fell to his knees on the sandy beach. First he thanked God. Then he claimed the land for the king and queen of Spain.

Columbus had landed on an island. He had not sailed to the Indies. He had not even come close to the Indies. But he had found lands that the people of Europe hadn't known about. He found the lands we now call the Americas.